GW01003292

How to Be More Confident: Tips for Increasing Self-Confidence

Daniel Payne

Published by Daniel Payne, 2024.

HOW TO BE MORE CONFIDENT: TIPS FOR INCREASING SELF-CONFIDENCE

First edition. February 18, 2024.

Copyright © 2024 Daniel Payne.

ISBN: 979-8224916399

Written by Daniel Payne.

Table of Contents

Don't Compare Yourself to Others

In today's society, it is incredibly common for individuals to compare themselves to others. With social media platforms like Instagram and Facebook constantly bombarding us with images of seemingly perfect lives, it is easy to fall into the trap of comparing ourselves to others. However, it is crucial to remember that everyone is on their own unique journey and that comparing ourselves to others serves no real purpose. In fact, it can be detrimental to our mental health and overall well-being.

When we compare ourselves to others, we are essentially measuring our own worth based on someone else's standards. This can lead to feelings of inadequacy, envy, and self-doubt. We may find ourselves constantly striving to meet unrealistic expectations or feeling like we are never good enough. This constant comparison can take a toll on our self-esteem and confidence, ultimately hindering our personal growth and happiness.

It is important to remember that everyone has their own strengths and weaknesses. Just because someone may seem to have it all together on the surface, it does not mean that they do not face their own struggles and insecurities. We are all human and no one is perfect. By focusing on our own journey and personal growth, we can better appreciate our own accomplishments and unique qualities.

Furthermore, comparing ourselves to others can also lead to a sense of entitlement or privilege. When we constantly measure our success based on someone else's achievements, we may lose sight of the hard work and dedication it took for them to get to where they are. This can lead to a lack of appreciation for our own efforts and a sense of entitlement that may not be justified.

It is also important to recognize that comparing ourselves to others is often an exercise in futility. Each person's journey is different and comparing ourselves to someone else's path is like comparing apples to oranges. We all have our own set of circumstances, challenges, and opportunities that shape who we are and where we are headed.

Instead of focusing on what others have or what they have accomplished, it is more beneficial to focus on our own goals and aspirations. By setting our own standards and benchmarks for success, we can better track our progress and work towards achieving our own personal best.

Moreover, constantly comparing ourselves to others can lead to a lack of self-awareness and self-acceptance. When we are so focused on what others have or do, we may lose sight of our own values, passions, and interests. It is important to cultivate a sense of self-awareness and self-acceptance in order to navigate our own path authentically and with purpose.

It is important to remember that comparing ourselves to others serves no real purpose. Everyone is on their own unique journey and no two paths are the same. By focusing on our own personal growth, achievements, and aspirations, we can better appreciate our own worth and live authentically. Embrace your individuality and remember that your worth is not determined by how you measure up to others, but by the unique qualities and strengths that make you who you are.

Self-Sabotage

S elf-sabotage is a common behavior that many individuals engage in, often without realizing the negative impact it has on their lives. It involves consciously or unconsciously engaging in behaviors that undermine one's own success, well-being, or goals. This can manifest in various ways, such as procrastination, negative self-talk, perfectionism, or fear of failure. While self-sabotage may seem like a coping mechanism in the moment, it ultimately prevents individuals from reaching their full potential and achieving their desired outcomes.

One of the key reasons why individuals engage in self-sabotage is fear. Fear of failure, fear of success, fear of rejection – these fears can paralyze individuals and prevent them from taking risks or pursuing their goals. By engaging in self-sabotaging behaviors, individuals are essentially protecting themselves from the possibility of experiencing discomfort, disappointment, or failure. However, by avoiding these perceived threats, individuals are also limiting their opportunities for growth, learning, and success.

Another common factor that contributes to self-sabotage is low self-esteem. Individuals who have low self-esteem may not believe that they are worthy of success or happiness, leading them to sabotage their efforts and undermine their own achievements. This negative self-perception can be reinforced by internalized beliefs, past experiences, or external judgments, creating a vicious cycle of self-sabotage and diminishing self-worth.

Perfectionism is another common trait that can fuel self-sabotage. Individuals who strive for perfection often set impossibly high standards for themselves and become overly critical of their own performance. This relentless pursuit of flawlessness can create a sense of never being good enough, leading individuals to engage in self-sabotaging behaviors as a way to cope with the pressure and anxiety of meeting unrealistic expectations.

Procrastination is also a prevalent form of self-sabotage that many individuals struggle with. By putting off tasks, delaying decisions, or avoiding responsibilities, individuals may sabotage their own progress and hinder their ability to achieve their goals. Procrastination is often rooted in fear, perfectionism, lack of motivation, or difficulty in managing time effectively, making it a challenging behavior to overcome.

In order to stop self-sabotage, individuals must first become aware of their patterns and triggers. This requires self-reflection, introspection, and a willingness to confront uncomfortable truths about oneself. By identifying the underlying reasons for engaging in self-sabotaging behaviors, individuals can begin to challenge and change their harmful thought patterns and habits.

Developing self-awareness and emotional intelligence is crucial in overcoming self-sabotage. By cultivating a deeper understanding of one's thoughts, feelings, and behaviors, individuals can gain insight into their motivations, fears, and insecurities. This self-awareness can help individuals develop healthier coping mechanisms, build resilience, and practice self-compassion in the face of setbacks or challenges.

Setting realistic goals and creating a structured plan for achieving them is essential in combating self-sabotage. By breaking down goals into manageable steps, setting deadlines, and holding oneself accountable, individuals can create a sense of purpose, direction, and momentum in their pursuits. By focusing on progress rather than perfection, individuals can alleviate the pressure of unrealistic expectations and reduce the temptation to engage in self-sabotaging behaviors.

Learning to embrace failure and view setbacks as opportunities for growth is crucial in stopping self-sabotage. By reframing failure as a natural part of the learning process, individuals can develop resilience, perseverance, and a growth mindset. Instead of punishing oneself for mistakes or setbacks, individuals can learn from them, adapt their strategies, and continue moving forward with renewed determination and resilience.

Seeking support from others, whether it be through therapy, coaching, or mentorship, can also be instrumental in overcoming self-sabotage. By sharing one's struggles, fears, and challenges with trusted individuals, individuals can receive guidance, perspective, and encouragement in navigating their obstacles and building their confidence. By building a supportive network of individuals who believe in one's potential and offer constructive feedback, individuals can strengthen their resilience and motivation in overcoming self-sabotage.

Self-sabotage is a harmful behavior that can hinder an individual's personal growth, success, and well-being. By recognizing the underlying causes of self-sabotaging behaviors, developing self-awareness and emotional intelligence, setting realistic goals, embracing failure, and seeking support, individuals can overcome self-sabotage.

Make Your Body a Temple

———

The phrase "make your body a temple" is often used to emphasize the importance of taking care of one's physical health and well-being. Just as a temple is a sacred and revered place, our bodies should also be treated with respect and care. This concept highlights the idea that our bodies are a precious gift that should be nourished and maintained in order to live a healthy and fulfilling life.

One of the key principles behind making your body a temple is the understanding that our bodies are intricately connected to our overall health and well-being. By nourishing our bodies with nutritious foods, engaging in regular exercise, and prioritizing self-care practices, we can enhance our physical, mental, and emotional health. This holistic approach to health recognizes the interconnectedness of our mind, body, and spirit, and emphasizes the importance of taking a comprehensive approach to self-care.

When we make our body a temple, we are investing in our long-term health and well-being. By adopting healthy habits and lifestyle choices, we can reduce our risk of developing chronic diseases such as heart disease, diabetes, and obesity. Regular exercise and physical activity can help improve cardiovascular health, strengthen muscles and bones, and boost overall energy levels. In addition, maintaining a balanced diet rich in fruits, vegetables, whole grains, and lean proteins can provide essential nutrients and antioxidants that support optimal health and function.

Furthermore, making your body a temple involves prioritizing mental and emotional well-being. Engaging in activities that promote relaxation, stress reduction, and emotional resilience can have profound effects on our overall health. Practicing mindfulness, meditation, and self-care techniques can help reduce anxiety, improve mood, and enhance emotional balance. It is important to recognize the impact that stress and negative emotions can have on our physical health, and to take proactive steps to manage our mental and emotional well-being.

Another important aspect of making your body a temple is taking care of your body's internal systems and organs. This includes staying hydrated, getting enough sleep, and avoiding harmful substances such as tobacco, alcohol, and drugs. Our bodies are incredibly resilient and adaptable, but they also require proper care and maintenance in order to function optimally. By prioritizing good sleep hygiene, staying hydrated, and avoiding harmful substances, we can support our body's natural detoxification processes and promote overall health and vitality.

In addition to physical health, making your body a temple also involves nurturing spiritual well-being. For many people, spirituality plays an important role in their overall health and well-being. Whether through prayer, meditation, or mindfulness practices, nurturing your spiritual side can provide a sense of purpose, meaning, and connection to something greater than yourself. This connection to a higher power or spiritual belief can help cultivate a sense of inner peace, resilience, and gratitude that can support overall health and well-being.

Making your body a temple is not just about physical health or appearance, but also about self-love and acceptance. Embracing your body and celebrating its unique strengths and capabilities can help foster a positive self-image and cultivate confidence and self-esteem. By practicing self-care and self-compassion, we can learn to treat ourselves with kindness and respect, and nurture a healthy relationship with our bodies.

Making your body a temple is a powerful and transformative concept that emphasizes the importance of prioritizing physical, mental, emotional, and spiritual well-being. By adopting healthy habits, engaging in self-care practices, and nurturing our bodies and minds with love and compassion, we can create a strong foundation for optimal health and vitality. Just as a temple is a sacred and revered place, our bodies should be treated with reverence and care, honoring the divine gift of life that resides within us. Let us strive to make our bodies temples of health, vitality, and wholeness, and live each day with gratitude and appreciation for the precious gift of our physical bodies.

Appearances

Taking pride in one's appearance is often viewed as a superficial concept, but in reality, it goes beyond just physical appearance and reflects one's self-respect and confidence. Maintaining a well-groomed and polished appearance can have a significant impact on how one is perceived by others and how they feel about themselves. It is an essential aspect of personal development and social interaction, as it can influence various aspects of one's life, including professional opportunities, social relationships, and self-esteem.

First and foremost, taking pride in one's appearance can have a positive impact on one's professional life. In many industries, the way one presents themselves can greatly affect their chances of success. Studies have shown that individuals who dress neatly and groom themselves well are often perceived as more competent and trustworthy by their colleagues and superiors. A well-groomed appearance can also boost one's confidence and sense of professionalism, which can lead to better job performance and career advancement opportunities.

Furthermore, maintaining a polished appearance can also have a positive impact on one's social relationships. The way we present ourselves can greatly influence how others perceive us and how they interact with us. People who take pride in their appearance are often seen as more approachable, likable, and confident, which can help in building strong and positive relationships with others. In social settings, a well-groomed appearance can also make a good impression on others, and can help in creating a positive image of oneself.

In addition to professional and social benefits, taking pride in one's appearance can also have a significant impact on one's self-esteem and mental well-being. When we take the time to groom ourselves well and present ourselves in a positive light, it can boost our self-confidence and self-worth. Feeling good about how we look can have a powerful effect on our mood and overall mental health, leading to a more positive outlook on life and increased resilience in the face of challenges.

Moreover, maintaining a polished appearance can also be a form of self-care and self-respect. By investing time and effort into grooming and dressing well, we are showing ourselves that we value and respect our own well-being. It is a way of expressing self-love and self-appreciation, and can contribute to a sense of self-empowerment and self-fulfillment. When we take pride in our appearance, we are sending a message to ourselves and to others that we are worth the effort, and that we deserve to look and feel our best.

Furthermore, taking pride in one's appearance can also be a form of personal expression and creativity. The way we present ourselves through our clothing, grooming, and personal style can be a reflection of our personality, interests, and values. It is a way of expressing ourselves to the world and showcasing our unique identity. By paying attention to our appearance and experimenting with different styles, we can explore and discover new aspects of ourselves, and develop a greater sense of self-awareness and self-expression.

In a society that often places a high value on physical appearance, taking pride in one's appearance can also be a form of empowerment and self-acceptance. By embracing and celebrating our unique features and taking care of our physical well-being, we are challenging societal norms and expectations, and reclaiming our own sense of beauty and self-worth. It is a way of showing that we are confident in who we are, and that we are comfortable in our own skin, regardless of societal standards or pressures.

Moreover, taking pride in one's appearance can also be a form of mindfulness and self-reflection. Grooming and dressing oneself can be a meditative and therapeutic practice that allows us to focus on the present moment and pay attention to our physical sensations and emotions. It can be a form of self-care that helps us connect with our bodies and minds, and cultivate a sense of presence and awareness. By taking the time to groom ourselves well and present ourselves in a positive light, we are engaging in a form of self-reflection and self-discovery that can lead to personal growth and inner transformation.

Furthermore, taking pride in one's appearance can also be a form of social responsibility and respect for others. When we present ourselves in a neat and well-groomed manner, we are showing consideration and respect for the people around us. It is a way of demonstrating our professionalism and courtesy in social interactions, and creating a positive and respectful environment for everyone. By taking care of our appearance, we are contributing to a foundation for self-confidence.

Procrastination

———

Procrastination is a common phenomenon that affects nearly everyone at some point in their lives. It is often easier to put off tasks that seem daunting or unappealing, even when we know they are important. However, procrastination can lead to increased stress, missed opportunities, and a sense of dissatisfaction with one's own productivity. Therefore, it is crucial to address and tackle tasks that we have been putting off. In this chapter, I will discuss the benefits of confronting procrastination and offer strategies for overcoming this common habit.

One of the key benefits of completing tasks that we have been putting off is a sense of accomplishment and satisfaction. By finally tackling that challenging project or difficult conversation, we can experience a boost in self-confidence and motivation. This can lead to increased productivity and a more positive outlook on future tasks. Additionally, completing tasks in a timely manner can prevent feelings of guilt or shame associated with procrastination, allowing us to focus on other priorities with a clear mind.

Furthermore, procrastination can have negative effects on our mental and emotional well-being. When we put off tasks, we may experience increased stress and anxiety as deadlines approach. This can lead to decreased performance and overall satisfaction with our work. By addressing tasks that we have been avoiding, we can alleviate these negative emotions and improve our mental health. This can also lead to improved relationships with others, as we may be more available and present when we are not overwhelmed by unfinished tasks.

In addition to the personal benefits of addressing procrastination, there are also practical advantages. By completing tasks in a timely manner, we can avoid missing deadlines and opportunities for advancement. This can lead to increased success in our academic, professional, and personal lives. Additionally, addressing tasks that we have been putting off can free up time and mental energy for other activities that bring us joy and fulfillment. By overcoming procrastination, we can create a more balanced and fulfilling life for ourselves.

There are several strategies that can help us overcome procrastination and tackle tasks that we have been putting off. One effective approach is to break tasks down into smaller, more manageable steps. By setting specific goals and deadlines for each step, we can create a sense of progress and momentum that can help us stay motivated.

Additionally, it can be helpful to identify any obstacles or challenges that may be preventing us from completing a task and develop a plan to address them. This can help us overcome procrastination and move forward with confidence.

Another helpful strategy for overcoming procrastination is to create a supportive environment that fosters productivity. This can include setting up a dedicated workspace, removing distractions, and establishing a routine that allows for focused work. By creating a conducive environment for completing tasks, we can increase our chances of success and reduce the temptation to procrastinate. Additionally, it can be helpful to seek support from others, such as friends, family, or colleagues, who can provide encouragement and accountability as we work towards our goals.

One of the most important aspects of overcoming procrastination is cultivating a positive mindset. Instead of focusing on past failures or missed opportunities, we can choose to approach tasks with a sense of curiosity and openness. By reframing our mindset from one of avoidance to one of engagement, we can increase our motivation and resilience in the face of challenges. This can help us overcome procrastination and achieve our goals with confidence and determination.

Addressing tasks that we have been putting off is a crucial step towards achieving our full potential and living a fulfilling life. Overcoming procrastination can lead to increased self-confidence, improved mental and emotional well-being, and practical benefits such as success in our academic, professional, and personal endeavors. By implementing strategies such as breaking tasks down into smaller steps, creating a supportive environment, and cultivating a positive mindset, we can overcome procrastination and take control of our productivity and happiness. It is never too late to address tasks that we have been avoiding – the benefits of doing so are well worth the effort.

Finding Inspiration

———

In a world that often feels chaotic and overwhelming, finding daily inspiration is essential for maintaining a sense of purpose and motivation. Whether it be in our personal or professional lives, having something or someone to look up to can help us stay focused and driven towards our goals. It is easy to get caught up in the demands of coursework and research, but finding daily inspiration can help us stay grounded and remind us of the bigger picture.

One way to find daily inspiration is through setting meaningful goals for ourselves. By establishing clear and achievable objectives, we can create a sense of purpose and direction in our lives. Whether it be completing a research project or mastering a new skill, having tangible goals to work towards can fuel our motivation and drive. Additionally, seeing progress towards our goals can provide a sense of accomplishment and satisfaction, further motivating us to continue moving forward.

Another source of daily inspiration can come from those around us. Surrounding ourselves with positive and uplifting individuals can help us stay motivated and inspired. Whether it be a mentor, a friend, or a colleague, having someone to support and encourage us can make a world of difference in our pursuit of success. By learning from the experiences and wisdom of others, we can gain valuable insights and perspectives that can help shape our own journey.

Engaging in activities that bring us joy and fulfillment can also serve as a source of daily inspiration. Whether it be through creative expression, physical activity, or meditation, finding time for activities that nourish our mind, body, and soul can help us stay inspired and motivated. Taking care of ourselves and prioritizing our well-being is essential for maintaining a positive outlook and a sense of purpose in our daily lives.

Reading books, watching documentaries, and consuming other forms of media can also provide us with daily inspiration. Learning about the accomplishments and struggles of others can help us gain perspective and insight into our own lives. By immersing ourselves in stories of resilience, perseverance, and triumph, we can find motivation and inspiration to overcome our own challenges and obstacles.

Reflecting on our past achievements and successes can also serve as a source of daily inspiration. By acknowledging and celebrating our accomplishments, no matter how big or small, we can boost our confidence and self-esteem. Remembering past moments of triumph can remind us of our capabilities and potential, motivating us to continue pushing ourselves towards new heights.

Finding daily inspiration can also come from within. By cultivating a positive mindset and practicing gratitude, we can tap into our inner reservoir of strength and motivation. Recognizing the blessings and opportunities in our lives can help us stay focused and inspired, even in the face of adversity. Cultivating a sense of optimism and resilience can help us navigate the challenges and uncertainties that come our way.

Setting aside time for reflection and introspection can also help us find daily inspiration. By pausing to reassess our values, beliefs, and goals, we can gain clarity and insight into what truly matters to us. Taking the time to listen to our inner voice and aligning our actions with our core values can provide us with a sense of purpose and direction in our daily lives.

Finding daily inspiration is essential for maintaining motivation and drive in our lives, especially as professional adults. Whether it be through setting meaningful goals, surrounding ourselves with positive influences, engaging in fulfilling activities, or reflecting on our past achievements, there are countless ways to find inspiration in our daily lives. By staying grounded and connected to our sources of inspiration, we can stay focused and driven towards our goals, even in the face of challenges and obstacles. Ultimately, finding daily inspiration is a powerful tool for unlocking our full potential and achieving success in all areas of our lives.

Cleanliness and Organization

———

Maintaining a clean and organized desk is essential for productivity and overall well-being in the workplace or at home. A cluttered desk can lead to distractions and decreased productivity, as it can be challenging to focus on tasks with a disorganized workspace. In addition, a messy desk can also contribute to feelings of stress and overwhelm, as the chaos surrounding us can affect our mental state.

One of the key benefits of maintaining a clean desk is improved efficiency. When everything is in its proper place and easily accessible, it becomes much easier to find what you need quickly and efficiently. This can save valuable time that would otherwise be wasted searching for misplaced items or sorting through piles of clutter. In a fast-paced work environment, time is a precious commodity, and anything that can help streamline tasks and processes is a valuable asset.

Furthermore, a clean desk can also have a positive impact on mental clarity and focus. When our workspace is neat and organized, it can help us feel more in control of our environment and reduce distractions. This can lead to improved concentration and productivity, as our minds are not constantly wandering to the mess around us. By creating a calming and orderly workspace, we are better able to focus on the task at hand and accomplish our goals more effectively.

Maintaining a clean desk also promotes professionalism and a positive impression on others. Whether it be clients, colleagues, or supervisors, a tidy workspace reflects well on your professionalism and attention to detail. People are more likely to respect and trust someone who takes pride in their appearance and surroundings, as it shows that they are organized and reliable. In a professional setting, first impressions are crucial, and a clean desk can help convey a sense of professionalism and competence.

From an environmental standpoint, maintaining a clean desk can also have a positive impact. By minimizing paper clutter and utilizing digital storage solutions, we can reduce our overall consumption of resources and waste. In today's digital age, it is important to consider the environmental implications of our actions and strive to minimize our carbon footprint whenever possible. By reducing our reliance on paper products and implementing eco-friendly practices, we can help contribute to a more sustainable future for our planet.

In addition to the practical benefits of maintaining a clean desk, there are also psychological advantages to consider. A cluttered workspace can contribute to feelings of stress and anxiety, as the chaos and disorganization can be overwhelming. By taking the time to declutter and organize our desk, we can create a more peaceful and calming environment that promotes mental well-being. A clean and tidy workspace can help us feel more relaxed and focused, leading to improved overall mental health and happiness.

One effective strategy for maintaining a clean desk is to establish a system for organizing and decluttering on a regular basis. This can involve setting aside time each day to tidy up and sort through items, as well as implementing systems for managing paperwork and digital files. By creating a routine for cleaning and organizing, we can prevent clutter from accumulating and ensure that our desk remains neat and orderly.

Another important aspect of maintaining a clean desk is to avoid unnecessary items and prioritize essentials. It can be all too easy to accumulate clutter by holding onto items that are no longer needed or relevant. By regularly assessing our workspace and removing items that are not essential, we can prevent unnecessary clutter and create a more streamlined and efficient workspace. This can also help to free up physical and mental space for more important tasks and activities.

Maintaining a clean and organized desk is crucial for productivity, mental well-being, and professionalism. By creating a clutter-free workspace, we can improve efficiency, focus, and overall happiness. In addition, a clean desk can have positive environmental implications by reducing waste and promoting sustainability. By establishing systems for organizing and decluttering, prioritizing essentials, and avoiding unnecessary items, we can create a workspace that is conducive to success and well-being. By taking the time to maintain our desk and environment, we can reap the benefits of a cleaner, calmer, and more productive workspace.

Appraising Ourselves

W e are constantly pushing ourselves to achieve new levels of knowledge and expertise in our chosen fields. However, it is equally important to take the time to reflect on our own strengths and weaknesses, and to appraise ourselves honestly. In this chapter, I will discuss the importance of self-appraisal, the benefits of recognizing our own abilities, and how we can use self-assessment to continue to grow and develop as scholars and professionals.

Self-appraisal is a crucial skill for everyone to develop, as it allows us to gain a better understanding of our own capabilities and limitations. By taking the time to reflect on our own performance, we can identify areas where we excel and areas where we may need to improve. This process of self-assessment can help us set realistic goals for ourselves and develop a plan for achieving them.

One of the benefits of appraising ourselves is that it can help us to build self-confidence and motivation. When we recognize our own strengths and accomplishments, we are more likely to feel confident in our abilities and motivated to continue working towards our goals. Conversely, when we acknowledge areas where we may need to improve, we can take steps to address those weaknesses and grow as scholars and professionals.

Self-appraisal can also help us to identify areas where we may need additional support or resources. For example, if we realize that we struggle with time management or organization, we can seek out workshops or coaching to help us improve in those areas. By being honest with ourselves about our needs and seeking out the necessary support, we can continue to grow and develop as individuals.

In addition to fostering self-awareness and personal growth, self-appraisal can also improve our communication and collaboration skills. When we have a better understanding of our own strengths and weaknesses, we can more effectively communicate our needs and preferences to others. This can lead to more productive collaborations and partnerships, both within our academic work and in our professional interactions.

Self-appraisal can also be a valuable tool for setting and achieving our academic and career goals. By evaluating our own performance and progress regularly, we can track our growth over time and make adjustments to our plans as needed. This can help us stay on track and continue moving towards our goals, even when faced with challenges or setbacks.

However, it is important to approach self-appraisal with a critical and objective mindset. It can be easy to overlook our weaknesses or inflate our accomplishments, but this type of self-deception will ultimately hinder our personal growth and development. Instead, we should strive to maintain a balanced perspective and be willing to acknowledge both our strengths and areas for improvement.

One way to ensure that our self-appraisal is as accurate and objective as possible is to seek feedback from others. Peers, mentors, and professors can provide valuable insights into our performance and help us identify blind spots or areas where we may need to improve. By soliciting feedback from others and listening openly to their perspectives, we can gain a more complete understanding of our own abilities and potential.

Self-appraisal is a critical skill for adults to develop in order to continue growing and developing as individuals and professionals. By honestly assessing our own abilities, recognizing our strengths and weaknesses, and seeking out feedback from others, we can set realistic goals, build self-confidence, and improve our communication and collaboration skills. Ultimately, self-appraisal is an ongoing process that can help us stay on track and continue moving towards our academic and career goals.

Seeking Feedback

———

As individuals strive for personal and professional growth, seeking feedback from trusted individuals is essential. A common misconception is that only seeking feedback from supervisors or mentors is necessary, but feedback can come from a variety of sources. Family, friends, colleagues, and even peers can provide valuable insights that can help individuals improve their skills, behaviors, and decision-making processes. By reaching out to those who know us best, we can gain a clearer understanding of our strengths and weaknesses, leading to a more successful and fulfilling life.

Trusted feedback can serve as a springboard for self-improvement. By actively seeking feedback from those who know us well, individuals can identify blind spots in their behavior or performance that may be hindering their progress. This feedback, when taken constructively, can lead to personal growth and development. For example, a colleague may offer feedback on a presentation style that can help an individual enhance their communication skills and become more effective in their professional interactions.

In addition to personal growth, seeking feedback from trusted individuals can also foster stronger relationships. When individuals take the time to ask for feedback and show that they are open to constructive criticism, it demonstrates a willingness to listen and learn. This open communication can lead to deeper connections and stronger bonds with those in our personal and professional circles. By engaging in a feedback loop with trusted individuals, we not only benefit from their perspectives but also strengthen our relationships in the process.

Trusted feedback can also be a valuable tool for decision-making. While seeking feedback from a variety of sources is important, the opinions of trusted individuals can carry more weight in the decision-making process. By gathering feedback from those who know us best, we can make more informed decisions that align with our values and goals. For example, seeking feedback from a close friend or family member before making a major career change can provide valuable insights that may not have been considered otherwise.

Another benefit of seeking feedback from trusted individuals is the opportunity to receive honest and constructive criticism. While feedback from supervisors or mentors can be helpful, it may be filtered or biased. Trusted individuals, on the other hand, are more likely to provide honest and unfiltered feedback that can help us see ourselves more clearly. By seeking feedback from those who have our best interests at heart, we can receive candid feedback that can help us grow and improve.

Ultimately, seeking feedback from trusted individuals can lead to increased self-awareness and self-improvement. By actively seeking feedback from those who know us best, we can gain a clearer understanding of our strengths and weaknesses. This self-awareness can help us identify areas for improvement and take steps to address them. In turn, self-improvement can lead to increased confidence, resilience, and success in all areas of our lives.

Seeking feedback from trusted individuals is a valuable practice that can lead to personal growth, stronger relationships, better decision-making, and increased self-awareness. By reaching out to those who know us best, we can gain valuable insights that can help us improve our skills, behaviors, and decision-making processes. Through active engagement in a feedback loop with trusted individuals, we can develop a clearer understanding of ourselves and take steps toward a more successful and fulfilling life. Asking for feedback from trusted people is a smart and strategic approach to personal and professional development that can lead to lasting benefits and positive outcomes.

Setting Goals

Setting goals is an essential aspect of both personal and professional development. Goals provide a sense of direction and purpose, helping individuals to focus their efforts and strive towards their objectives. Setting goals allows individuals to define what they want to achieve, create a roadmap for success, and measure their progress along the way. In order to effectively set and achieve goals, it is important to establish clear and specific objectives that are challenging yet attainable.

When setting goals, it is important to consider both short-term and long-term objectives. Short-term goals provide immediate targets to work towards, while long-term goals offer a broader perspective and vision for the future. By setting both short-term and long-term goals, individuals can create a balanced and comprehensive plan for success. Short-term goals can serve as stepping stones towards achieving larger, more ambitious long-term goals.

In addition to setting clear objectives, it is important to establish a timeline for achieving goals. By setting deadlines and milestones, individuals can track their progress and make adjustments as needed. Timelines help individuals stay focused and motivated, providing a sense of urgency and accountability. Setting deadlines also helps to prioritize tasks and allocate resources effectively.

Setting goals also requires a certain level of self-awareness and introspection. It is important to identify strengths, weaknesses, opportunities, and threats when defining goals. By understanding personal limitations and potential obstacles, individuals can develop strategies to overcome challenges and maximize their chances of success. Self-awareness allows individuals to set realistic and achievable goals that align with their values, interests, and capabilities.

Furthermore, setting goals requires commitment and dedication. Achieving goals requires consistent effort and perseverance, as well as the ability to adapt to changing circumstances. It is important to stay motivated and focused on the end goal, even when facing setbacks or obstacles. By maintaining a positive attitude and a growth mindset, individuals can overcome challenges and achieve their goals.

Setting goals also involves effective planning and organization. Individuals must develop a structured plan of action, outlining the steps needed to achieve their objectives. By breaking down goals into smaller, manageable tasks, individuals can create a roadmap for success and track their progress over time. Planning and organization help individuals stay on track and make progress towards their goals in a systematic and efficient manner.

Moreover, setting goals can help individuals to measure their success and celebrate their achievements. By setting benchmarks and milestones, individuals can track their progress and evaluate their performance. Achieving goals provides a sense of accomplishment and satisfaction, boosting confidence and motivation. Celebrating successes along the way can also help individuals stay motivated and continue striving towards their goals.

Setting goals is a crucial component of personal and professional development. Goals provide direction, purpose, and motivation, helping individuals to focus their efforts and work towards their objectives. By setting clear and specific goals, establishing timelines and deadlines, developing self-awareness and commitment, and creating a structured plan of action, individuals can achieve success and realize their full potential. Setting goals requires dedication, perseverance, and a positive mindset, as well as the ability to adapt to changing circumstances and overcome obstacles. Ultimately, setting goals can lead to personal growth, fulfillment, and success in all areas of life.

Planning

Planning your life direction and route is essential for achieving success and fulfillment in both personal and professional endeavors. It involves setting clear goals and objectives, identifying potential obstacles, and creating a roadmap to navigate through life's challenges and opportunities. Just like a GPS guides you to your destination, having a plan for your life helps you stay focused and on track towards reaching your desired destination.

The first step in planning your life direction and route is to set specific, measurable, achievable, relevant, and time-bound (SMART) goals. By clearly defining what you want to achieve and when you want to achieve it, you can create a roadmap to guide you towards success. Whether it's earning a degree, starting a business, or improving your health, having concrete goals gives you a sense of purpose and direction.

Once you have established your goals, the next step is to identify potential obstacles and challenges that may hinder your progress. By anticipating potential roadblocks, you can proactively plan ways to overcome them and stay on course towards your goals. This may involve seeking support from mentors, developing new skills, or changing your approach to reach your goals more effectively.

In addition to setting goals and identifying obstacles, it is important to create a detailed plan of action to help you achieve your objectives. This involves breaking down your goals into smaller, manageable tasks and creating a timeline for completing each task. By taking small, consistent steps towards your goals, you can make progress and stay motivated along the way.

Furthermore, it is crucial to regularly review and adjust your plan as needed. Life is unpredictable, and circumstances may change over time. By regularly assessing your progress and adjusting your plan accordingly, you can stay agile and adapt to new opportunities or challenges that may arise.

In addition to creating a plan for your professional goals, it is also important to consider your personal goals and overall well-being. This may involve setting goals related to health, relationships, personal development, or work-life balance. By balancing both personal and professional goals, you can create a harmonious and fulfilling life that aligns with your values and priorities.

Furthermore, it is important to seek feedback and support from others as you plan your life direction and route. By sharing your goals and aspirations with trusted friends, family members, or mentors, you can gain valuable insights and perspectives that may help you refine your plan and stay motivated.

Moreover, it is important to stay motivated and focused on your goals, even when faced with setbacks or challenges. By staying positive, resilient, and committed to your goals, you can overcome obstacles and stay on course towards achieving success and fulfillment in your life.

Planning your life direction and route is a critical component of achieving success and fulfillment in both personal and professional endeavors. By setting clear goals, identifying obstacles, creating a roadmap, and regularly reviewing and adjusting your plan, you can navigate through life's challenges and opportunities with purpose and grace. With determination, resilience, and a strategic plan in place, you can create a life that aligns with your values, aspirations, and dreams.

Body Language

Body language plays a crucial role in portraying confidence. It is often said that actions speak louder than words, and this is particularly true when it comes to exuding confidence. The way we hold ourselves, our gestures, and facial expressions all contribute to how others perceive us. By mastering effective body language, individuals can project confidence and credibility in various social and professional settings.

One key aspect of body language for confidence is maintaining good posture. Standing tall with shoulders back and head held high signals strength and self-assurance. Slouching or hunching over can give the impression of insecurity and lack of confidence. By consciously making an effort to improve posture, individuals can instantly appear more confident and assertive.

Eye contact is another important aspect of body language that reflects confidence. Making direct eye contact with others shows that you are engaged and attentive. Avoiding eye contact can be perceived as shyness or discomfort. By maintaining steady eye contact, individuals can convey confidence and sincerity in their interactions.

Gestures and hand movements also play a significant role in body language for confidence. Using open and expansive gestures can convey confidence and enthusiasm. Conversely, fidgeting or excessive hand movements can suggest nervousness or lack of confidence. By being mindful of their gestures, individuals can present themselves as confident and poised.

Facial expressions are another crucial element of body language for confidence. Smiling and maintaining a pleasant expression can make others feel at ease and signal approachability. On the other hand, a scowling or tense facial expression can give off negative vibes and undermine confidence. By keeping a friendly and positive demeanor, individuals can radiate confidence and charm.

Confident body language also involves controlling nervous habits and mannerisms. Tapping feet, biting nails, or twirling hair can convey anxiety and insecurity. By practicing mindfulness and being aware of these habits, individuals can project a more composed and confident image. It is important to cultivate self-awareness and address any nervous tics that may detract from one's confidence.

Mirroring is a powerful technique in body language that can enhance feelings of rapport and confidence in social interactions. Mirroring involves subtly imitating the gestures and body language of others, which can help create a sense of connection and understanding. By mirroring the body language of confident individuals, one can adopt similar postures and gestures to project confidence themselves.

Confident body language also involves using space effectively. Standing too close to others can come across as invasive or aggressive, while standing too far away can create distance and detachment. By striking a balance and maintaining an appropriate distance, individuals can convey confidence and respect in their interactions. Being mindful of personal space can help build positive relationships and enhance one's overall confidence.

Another important aspect of body language for confidence is maintaining a calm and composed demeanor. Speaking slowly and clearly, using a steady tone of voice, and avoiding nervous gestures can all contribute to projecting confidence. By exuding a sense of calm and control in their body language, individuals can inspire trust and credibility in others.

Body language plays a crucial role in projecting confidence and credibility. By mastering the art of effective body language, individuals can enhance their self-confidence and make a positive impression on others. From posture and eye contact to gestures and facial expressions, every aspect of body language contributes to how we are perceived by others. By practicing and refining their body language skills, individuals can exude confidence and assertiveness in various social and professional settings. Ultimately, understanding and mastering body language for confidence can empower individuals to achieve their goals and succeed in their personal and professional endeavors.

Role Models

Having a role model is an integral part of personal and professional development. A role model is someone we look up to, admire, and seek to emulate in various aspects of our lives. Finding a role model can provide us with inspiration, motivation, and direction. It is important to choose a role model who possesses characteristics or traits that align with our own values and goals. When selecting a role model, it is essential to consider their achievements, actions, and impact on society.

One of the key benefits of having a role model is the guidance and support they can provide. A role model can serve as a mentor, offering valuable advice and insight based on their own experiences and successes. By observing how our role model approaches challenges, makes decisions, and handles adversity, we can gain valuable lessons and perspectives that can help us navigate our own paths more effectively. In this way, a role model can act as a source of wisdom and guidance in our personal and professional lives.

Another important aspect of having a role model is the inspiration they can provide. A role model can serve as a source of motivation, showing us what is possible through hard work, dedication, and perseverance. By witnessing the achievements of our role model, we can be inspired to set higher goals for ourselves and strive for excellence in our own endeavors. This motivation can help us push past our limits, overcome obstacles, and reach our full potential.

Moreover, a role model can also help us develop important qualities and characteristics that are essential for success. By observing the behaviors and attitudes of our role model, we can learn important lessons in leadership, resilience, and integrity. A role model can serve as a positive influence, encouraging us to cultivate virtues such as honesty, determination, and compassion. By emulating the positive qualities of our role model, we can improve ourselves and become better individuals in the process.

Furthermore, having a role model can help us expand our horizons and explore new possibilities. A role model can expose us to different perspectives, ideas, and opportunities that we may not have considered otherwise. By learning from our role model's experiences and achievements, we can broaden our own knowledge and understanding of the world. This exposure can help us think outside the box, challenge our assumptions, and develop a more expansive view of our own potential.

Additionally, having a role model can provide us with a sense of direction and purpose in life. A role model can help us clarify our goals, ambitions, and values, guiding us towards a more fulfilling and meaningful future. By aligning our aspirations with those of our role model, we can create a roadmap for success and set ourselves on a path towards personal growth and fulfillment. This sense of purpose can give us the motivation and drive to pursue our dreams with passion and determination.

Finding a role model is a crucial step in our personal and professional development. A role model can offer us guidance, inspiration, and support as we navigate the challenges of life and strive for success. By choosing a role model who embodies qualities and values that resonate with our own, we can learn important lessons, expand our horizons, and develop the skills necessary for personal growth and fulfillment. Ultimately, having a role model can empower us to become the best version of ourselves and achieve our goals with confidence and determination.

Hypnotherapy

Hypnotherapy is a form of therapy that utilizes hypnosis to achieve a state of focused attention and heightened suggestibility in order to facilitate positive changes in behavior, thoughts, and feelings. It has been used for a variety of purposes, including smoking cessation, weight loss, and stress reduction, but one particularly beneficial application of hypnotherapy is for boosting confidence. Confidence is a crucial quality that can greatly impact an individual's success and well-being in all aspects of life. Whether it be in personal relationships, professional endeavors, or even just day-to-day interactions, having confidence can make a world of difference.

Many people struggle with feelings of self-doubt and insecurity, which can hold them back from reaching their full potential. Hypnotherapy for confidence aims to address these issues by helping individuals tap into their inner strength and belief in themselves. During a hypnotherapy session, the therapist will guide the individual into a state of deep relaxation and focus, allowing them to access their subconscious mind where beliefs and behaviors are stored. Through suggestion and visualization techniques, the therapist can help the individual reframe negative thought patterns and replace them with positive beliefs and affirmations.

Research has shown that hypnotherapy can be an effective tool for building confidence. A study published in the Journal of

Consulting and Clinical Psychology found that participants who received hypnotherapy for confidence experienced significant improvements in self-esteem and assertiveness compared to those in a control group. This suggests that hypnotherapy can help individuals overcome their limiting beliefs and develop a more positive self-image.

One of the key benefits of hypnotherapy for confidence is that it can provide lasting results. Unlike other forms of therapy that may require ongoing sessions or maintenance, hypnotherapy can create lasting changes in a relatively short amount of time. This is because hypnosis targets the subconscious mind, where beliefs and behaviors are deeply ingrained, making it easier to reprogram negative thought patterns and create new, more empowering beliefs.

In addition to boosting confidence, hypnotherapy can also help individuals overcome specific fears and phobias that may be holding them back. For example, someone who has a fear of public speaking may benefit from hypnotherapy to build their confidence and overcome their anxiety. By addressing these specific issues through hypnotherapy, individuals can gain the tools and techniques needed to navigate challenging situations with confidence and ease.

Furthermore, hypnotherapy for confidence is a safe and non-invasive treatment option that can be tailored to suit each individual's needs and goals. Unlike medication or other conventional therapies, hypnotherapy has no known side effects and is generally well-tolerated by most people. This makes it an appealing option for those looking to boost their confidence without the use of pharmaceuticals or invasive procedures.

It is important to note that hypnotherapy is not a quick fix or a magic solution for all confidence issues. It is a process that requires commitment and effort on the part of the individual. It is also important to work with a qualified and experienced hypnotherapist who can guide you through the process and ensure that you are receiving the best care possible. By approaching hypnotherapy with an open mind and a willingness to change, individuals can unlock their true potential and cultivate a sense of confidence that will serve them well in all areas of life.

Hypnotherapy for confidence is a powerful and effective tool for building self-esteem, overcoming fears, and achieving personal growth. By tapping into the subconscious mind and rewiring negative thought patterns, individuals can cultivate a deep sense of self-assurance and belief in themselves. With the guidance of a skilled hypnotherapist, individuals can embark on a transformative journey towards greater confidence and self-empowerment. Through dedication, patience, and a willingness to change, individuals can unlock their full potential and thrive in all areas of life.

Comfort Zones

S tepping out of one's comfort zone is an important aspect of personal growth and development. This is particularly relevant in the context of gaining confidence, where individuals are constantly faced with new challenges and opportunities for learning. While it may be tempting to stick to familiar routines and habits, pushing oneself to try new things can lead to invaluable experiences and insights.

One of the main reasons why it is important to get out of one's comfort zone is that it fosters personal growth. When individuals try new things or take on new challenges, they are forced to adapt and learn new skills. This not only helps to broaden one's knowledge and capabilities but also enhances their resilience and ability to cope with uncertainty. In life in general, where things are constantly evolving, being open to stepping out of one's comfort zone can be instrumental in navigating the challenges that come with pursuing advanced education.

Moreover, stepping out of one's comfort zone can lead to increased creativity and innovation. By exposing oneself to new experiences and perspectives, individuals can gain fresh insights and ideas that can inform their work and research. This can be particularly beneficial for those seeking to gain confidence. By pushing themselves to try new things and explore unfamiliar terrain, any person can develop a more innovative approach to their academic pursuits.

Another reason why it is important to get out of one's comfort zone is that it can enhance one's communication and collaboration skills. In life, where individuals are often required to work in teams or collaborate with colleagues from diverse backgrounds, being open to stepping out of one's comfort zone can facilitate effective communication and cooperation. By challenging oneself to engage with different perspectives and approaches, you can develop a greater understanding of others and improve their ability to work effectively in a team setting.

Furthermore, stepping out of one's comfort zone can help to build confidence and self-efficacy. By pushing oneself to try new things and take on new challenges, individuals can prove to themselves that they are capable of overcoming obstacles and achieving their goals. This can be particularly valuable in any area of life, where the demands can be high and the pressure to succeed can be intense. By stepping out of their comfort zone and pushing themselves beyond their limits, people can build the confidence and resilience needed to thrive in a competitive academic environment.

In addition, stepping out of one's comfort zone can lead to increased adaptability and flexibility. In the modern world, where individuals are constantly faced with changing circumstances and shifting priorities, being open to trying new things and exploring unfamiliar territory can help to build the resilience and adaptability needed to navigate the challenges associated with daily life. By pushing themselves to step out of their comfort zone, people can develop the flexibility and agility required to respond effectively to the demands of their academic pursuits.

Moreover, stepping out of one's comfort zone can foster a sense of curiosity and intellectual exploration. By exposing oneself to new experiences and perspectives, individuals can develop a deeper understanding of the world around them and expand their intellectual horizons. In the school of life, where the pursuit of knowledge and understanding is a central goal, being open to stepping out of one's comfort zone can help students to engage more deeply with their interests and explore new avenues of research and inquiry.

Stepping out of one's comfort zone can lead to increased resilience and perseverance. By pushing oneself to try new things and take on new challenges, individuals can develop the resilience and determination needed to overcome obstacles and setbacks. This can be particularly important in adult life, where the road to success can be long and arduous. By stepping out of their comfort zone and pushing themselves to persevere in the face of adversity, individuals can develop the resilience and determination needed to succeed in all of their pursuits.

Stepping out of one's comfort zone is an essential aspect of personal growth and development, particularly in the context of gaining confidence. By challenging oneself to try new things and explore unfamiliar terrain, individuals can broaden their knowledge, enhance their creativity, improve their communication skills, build confidence, increase adaptability, foster curiosity, and develop resilience. In the competitive and fast-paced world of adulthood, being open to stepping out of one's comfort zone can be key to thriving in the face of challenges and achieving success. So, embrace the unknown, challenge yourself, and push the boundaries of your comfort zone to unlock your full potential as an individual with inherent worth and value.

Helping Others

In a world that often prioritizes individualism and self-interest, the act of offering to help others can be a powerful and transformative gesture. This act reflects a deep sense of empathy, altruism, and compassion towards those around us. When we extend a helping hand to others, we not only contribute to their well-being and happiness but also cultivate a sense of community and interconnectedness. In this chapter, I will explore the significance of offering to help others, the benefits it brings to both the giver and the receiver, and the ways in which we can incorporate this practice into our daily lives.

One of the key reasons why offering to help others is important is that it reflects our innate sense of humanity and our capacity for empathy. By reaching out to others in times of need, we show that we care about their well-being and are willing to support them in any way we can. This act of kindness can have a profound impact on the recipient, helping them feel valued, understood, and supported. Moreover, offering to help others can also foster a sense of connection and belonging, creating a strong bond between individuals and strengthening the fabric of our communities.

Furthermore, offering to help others can also bring about personal growth and development. When we extend a helping hand to someone in need, we challenge ourselves to step outside of our comfort zones, broaden our perspectives, and expand our horizons. This act of service enables us to develop important skills such as empathy, communication, problem-solving, and collaboration, which are essential for building strong relationships and navigating the complexities of the world. By offering to help others, we not only strengthen our emotional intelligence but also cultivate a sense of purpose and fulfillment in our lives.

In addition, offering to help others can also have a positive impact on our mental and emotional well-being. Research has shown that acts of kindness and generosity towards others can boost our mood, reduce stress levels, and improve our overall sense of happiness and satisfaction. When we offer to help others, we experience a sense of fulfillment, gratitude, and connection that can help us overcome feelings of loneliness, isolation, and negativity. By engaging in acts of service and selflessness, we can cultivate a positive mindset and create a ripple effect of kindness and compassion in our lives.

Moreover, offering to help others can also promote a sense of social responsibility and civic engagement. By taking the initiative to support those in need, we contribute to the common good and work towards creating a more caring, inclusive, and equitable society. When we extend a helping hand to others, we not only address immediate needs and challenges but also foster a culture of solidarity, reciprocity, and cooperation. This act of service can inspire others to do the same, creating a ripple effect of positive change that benefits everyone in the community.

Additionally, offering to help others can also foster a sense of gratitude and appreciation for the things we have in our lives. When we take the time to reach out to those in need, we become more aware of the privileges, opportunities, and resources that we often take for granted. This act of service can help us cultivate a sense of humility, empathy, and gratitude, encouraging us to give back to the community and make a positive impact in the lives of others. By offering to help others, we not only express our gratitude for the blessings we have received but also create a more compassionate and caring society for everyone.

Furthermore, offering to help others can also strengthen our interpersonal relationships and build a sense of trust and connection with those around us. When we extend a helping hand to someone in need, we show that we are reliable, compassionate, and supportive, creating a strong foundation for meaningful and fulfilling relationships. This act of kindness can help us build a sense of trust, respect, and empathy with others, fostering a deep sense of connection and understanding that can withstand the test of time. By offering to help others, we can strengthen our social bonds and create a network of support and solidarity that enriches our lives and those of others.

Moreover, offering to help others can also promote a sense of empowerment and agency in our lives. When we take the initiative to support those in need, we demonstrate our ability to make a positive impact and bring about meaningful change in the world. This act of service enables us to use our skills, resources, and talents for the greater good, empowering us to become agents of positive transformation and social change. By offering to help others, we can harness our potential and create a more just society.

It's OK to be Introverted

In today's society, extroversion is often celebrated and seen as necessary for success, but the reality is that introverts possess unique strengths and abilities that are often overlooked. However, becoming a powerful introvert is not necessarily about changing who you are, but rather embracing and harnessing those introverted qualities to achieve personal and professional success. This chapter will explore the characteristics of introverts, the challenges they face in a society that values extroversion, and strategies for becoming a powerful introvert.

Introverts are individuals who tend to be more reserved, reflective, and independent. They often prefer solitude and quiet environments, and are energized by spending time alone or in small groups. Introverts are deep thinkers, often processing information internally before sharing their thoughts with others. They are also known for their creativity, empathy, and ability to listen deeply and carefully. These qualities make introverts valuable contributors in many different areas of life, from the arts to business to academia.

Despite their strengths, introverts can face challenges in a society that values extroversion. Introverts may be seen as aloof, shy, or lacking in social skills, which can lead to misunderstandings and missed opportunities. In addition, introverts may feel pressure to conform to extroverted expectations in social and professional settings, which can be exhausting and draining for them.

However, by understanding their own strengths and preferences, introverts can learn to navigate these challenges and leverage their unique qualities to achieve success.

One strategy for becoming a powerful introvert is to cultivate self-awareness and self-acceptance. This involves recognizing and appreciating your introverted qualities, such as your ability to listen, your creativity, and your deep thinking. It also involves understanding your own limits and boundaries, and learning to assertively communicate your needs and preferences to others. By developing a strong sense of self-awareness and self-acceptance, introverts can build confidence in their abilities and navigate social and professional situations more effectively.

Another strategy for becoming a powerful introvert is to focus on developing and honing your strengths. Introverts are often gifted in areas such as writing, research, and analysis, so it can be beneficial to cultivate these skills and pursue opportunities that allow you to excel in these areas. Introverts can also benefit from developing their communication skills, such as public speaking, networking, and assertiveness, which can help them to navigate social and professional situations more confidently. By focusing on their strengths and areas of interest, introverts can build a successful and fulfilling career that aligns with their natural tendencies.

Networking is an important aspect of professional success, but it can be challenging for introverts who may find large social events overwhelming and draining. However, introverts can still build effective professional networks by focusing on quality over quantity. Instead of trying to attend every networking event, introverts can choose smaller, more intimate gatherings where they can engage in deeper conversations and connections. Introverts can also leverage their listening skills and empathy to build meaningful relationships with colleagues, mentors, and clients. By approaching networking in a thoughtful and strategic way, introverts can build a strong professional network that supports their career growth.

Time management is another important factor in becoming a powerful introvert. Introverts often need time alone to recharge and process information, so it's important to prioritize self-care and downtime in your schedule. By scheduling regular breaks, setting boundaries around your time and energy, and practicing mindfulness and relaxation techniques, introverts can manage their energy levels and prevent burnout. By taking care of yourself and your needs, you can show up as your best self in social and professional situations, and achieve success on your own terms.

Another way for introverts to become powerful is to challenge themselves and step out of their comfort zone. While introverts may prefer solitude and quiet environments, it's important for personal and professional growth to push yourself to try new things and take on challenges. This could involve speaking up in meetings, volunteering for leadership opportunities, or participating in group projects. By stepping out of your comfort zone and trying new experiences, introverts can build confidence, develop new skills, and expand their comfort zone over time. By embracing discomfort and pushing yourself to grow, you can become a more powerful and confident introvert.

Becoming a powerful introvert is not about changing who you are, but about embracing and harnessing your unique qualities to achieve personal and professional success. Introverts possess valuable strengths such as deep thinking, creativity, and empathy

Relax

In our fast-paced and demanding world, it can be easy to forget the importance of allowing oneself to relax. However, relaxation is not just a luxury or a treat; it is a vital component of maintaining mental, physical, and emotional well-being. When we allow ourselves to relax, we give our bodies and minds the opportunity to rest, recharge, and rejuvenate. This can improve our overall health, productivity, and quality of life.

One of the key benefits of relaxation is stress reduction. When we are constantly on the go and under pressure, our bodies release stress hormones such as cortisol, which can have negative effects on our health. By taking the time to relax, we can lower our stress levels and reduce the risk of developing stress-related illnesses such as heart disease, high blood pressure, and depression.

Relaxation also allows us to improve our focus and concentration. When we are constantly multitasking and juggling numerous responsibilities, our minds can become overwhelmed and exhausted. Taking the time to relax can help clear our minds and improve our ability to focus on tasks at hand. This can lead to increased productivity and better performance in our work or studies.

Furthermore, relaxation can have a positive impact on our relationships. When we are constantly stressed and irritable, it can affect our interactions with others and lead to conflicts and misunderstandings. By taking the time to relax and de-stress, we can improve our mood, communication, and overall interactions with those around us. This can help strengthen our relationships and foster a sense of connection and support.

In addition, relaxation can improve our physical health. When we are stressed, our bodies can experience a range of negative effects such as muscle tension, headaches, and digestive issues. By allowing ourselves to relax, we can reduce these physical symptoms and promote better overall health. Relaxation techniques such as deep breathing, meditation, and yoga can help lower blood pressure, reduce muscle tension, and improve immune function.

Another important benefit of relaxation is improved sleep. When we are stressed and anxious, it can be difficult to fall asleep and stay asleep. By taking the time to relax before bed, we can calm our minds and bodies, making it easier to drift off to sleep and experience deeper, more restful rest. This can lead to improved energy levels, mood, and overall well-being.

Furthermore, relaxation can help us cope with difficult emotions and experiences. When we are faced with challenges and setbacks, it can be easy to become overwhelmed and discouraged. By taking the time to relax and practice self-care, we can strengthen our resilience and ability to cope with stress and adversity. This can help us navigate difficult situations with a sense of calm and perspective.

Moreover, relaxation can foster creativity and inspiration. When our minds are constantly busy and preoccupied, it can be difficult to tap into our creative potential and come up with new ideas. By allowing ourselves to relax and unwind, we give our minds the freedom to wander, explore, and innovate. This can lead to fresh insights, perspectives, and solutions to problems or challenges we may be facing.

Additionally, relaxation can improve our overall sense of well-being and happiness. When we are constantly stressed and overwhelmed, it can be difficult to experience joy and contentment in our lives. By taking the time to relax and engage in activities that bring us pleasure and fulfillment, we can enhance our overall quality of life. This can lead to increased feelings of gratitude, satisfaction, and fulfillment.

Relaxation is not just a luxury; it is a necessity for maintaining our health, happiness, and overall well-being. By allowing ourselves to relax, we can reduce stress, improve focus, strengthen relationships, and promote physical health. Relaxation can also help us cope with difficult emotions, foster creativity, and enhance our overall sense of well-being. So, take the time to unwind, recharge, and allow yourself to relax. Your mind, body, and spirit will thank you for it.

Saying No

———

Learning to say no is a skill that many people struggle with, yet it is vital for maintaining healthy boundaries and managing one's time and energy effectively. Saying no can be difficult, especially for individuals who are accustomed to saying yes to every request or invitation that comes their way. However, learning to say no is an essential aspect of self-care and can help prevent burnout, overwhelm, and resentment in both personal and professional relationships. In this chapter, we will explore the importance of saying no, the challenges that may arise when doing so, and strategies for effectively asserting boundaries and prioritizing one's own needs and well-being.

One of the key reasons why it is important to learn to say no is that it allows individuals to set boundaries and prioritize their own needs and well-being. By saying no to things that do not align with their values, goals, and priorities, individuals can prevent themselves from becoming overcommitted, overwhelmed, and stressed. Saying no can also help individuals protect their time and energy, allowing them to focus on activities and relationships that are most important to them. In this way, saying no is an act of self-care and self-preservation that can help individuals maintain balance and harmony in their lives.

However, saying no can be challenging for many people, especially those who are people-pleasers or who have difficulty asserting themselves. The fear of disappointing others, being viewed as selfish or uncooperative, or missing out on opportunities can make it difficult for individuals to say no when necessary. Additionally, saying no can be uncomfortable or anxiety-provoking, especially if individuals are not used to setting boundaries or advocating for themselves. Despite these challenges, it is important for individuals to overcome their fear of saying no and learn to assert their boundaries assertively and confidently.

One strategy for learning to say no is to practice assertiveness and communication skills. Individuals can benefit from learning how to communicate their needs, desires, and boundaries clearly and directly, without feeling guilty or apologizing for their decisions. By practicing assertive communication, individuals can improve their ability to say no in a respectful and considerate manner, while also remaining firm and confident in their choices. Additionally, individuals can benefit from setting clear priorities and boundaries, so that they can easily discern when it is necessary to say no to certain requests or demands.

Another strategy for learning to say no is to reflect on one's values, goals, and priorities. By clarifying what is most important to them and what they want to focus their time and energy on, individuals can make more informed decisions about when to say no. By aligning their choices with their values and goals, individuals can feel more confident and empowered in asserting their boundaries and prioritizing their own well-being. Reflecting on one's values can also help individuals cultivate a greater sense of self-awareness and self-compassion, making it easier for them to say no when necessary.

In addition to practicing assertiveness, communication skills, and reflecting on one's values, individuals can benefit from seeking support and guidance from trusted friends, family members, or mental health professionals. Talking to others about one's struggles with saying no can help individuals gain insight, perspective, and encouragement to overcome their fear and resistance to setting boundaries. Trusted individuals can also provide feedback, strategies, and accountability to help individuals practice asserting themselves and saying no in a healthy and effective way. By seeking support from others, individuals can feel less alone and more empowered to prioritize their needs and well-being.

Overall, learning to say no is an essential skill that can help individuals protect their time and energy, set boundaries, and prioritize their own well-being. Despite the challenges that may arise when saying no, individuals can benefit from practicing assertiveness, communication skills, and self-reflection, while also seeking support and guidance from others. By learning to say no in a respectful and considerate manner, individuals can prevent burnout, overwhelm, and resentment, and instead cultivate balance, harmony, and self-care in their lives. Through self-awareness, courage, and perseverance, individuals can learn to say no when necessary, and ultimately create a more fulfilling and authentic life for themselves.

Don't Give Up

In life, there are countless challenges and obstacles that we encounter on a daily basis. Whether it be personal struggles, academic setbacks, or unforeseen circumstances, it is easy to feel overwhelmed and defeated. However, in times of hardship, it is crucial to remember the importance of perseverance and resilience. The phrase "don't give up" serves as a powerful reminder that no matter how difficult the situation may seem, there is always hope and potential for success. This chapter will explore the significance of pushing through adversity, the benefits of resilience, and the mindset required to overcome obstacles.

One of the key reasons why it is important to not give up in the face of adversity is that success often lies just beyond the point where most people would have quit. Many great achievements in history have been the result of individuals who refused to give up, even when faced with seemingly insurmountable challenges. For example, Thomas Edison famously failed over a thousand times before successfully inventing the light bulb. If he had given up after the first few attempts, the world may never have seen his groundbreaking invention.

Furthermore, giving up can have long-term negative consequences on one's mental well-being and self-esteem. When we repeatedly quit in the face of adversity, we reinforce a pattern of failure that can be difficult to break. Conversely, pushing through challenges and overcoming obstacles can build resilience and self-confidence. By persevering in the face of adversity, we learn valuable lessons about our own capabilities and strengths, which can help us tackle future challenges with greater ease.

In addition, resilience is a key characteristic that is highly valued in today's society. Employers seek individuals who can adapt to change, problem solve, and persevere in the face of challenges. By demonstrating resilience and determination in the face of adversity, we not only increase our own chances of success but also set a positive example for others. In a world that is constantly evolving and changing, the ability to bounce back from setbacks is a valuable skill that can set us apart from others.

Moreover, the phrase "don't give up" serves as a powerful reminder of the importance of having a growth mindset. In her book, "Mindset: The New Psychology of Success," psychologist Carol Dweck discusses the concept of fixed mindset versus growth mindset. Individuals with a fixed mindset believe that their abilities are predetermined and static, while those with a growth mindset believe that they can improve and grow through effort and perseverance. By embracing a growth mindset and refusing to give up in the face of challenges, we open ourselves up to greater opportunities for personal and professional growth.

It is also important to acknowledge that giving up is a choice, and that we have the power to choose perseverance over defeat. While it may be tempting to throw in the towel when faced with adversity, it is important to remember that every setback is an opportunity for growth and learning. By choosing to push through challenges and not give up, we demonstrate our commitment to our goals and aspirations, and show ourselves that we are capable of overcoming even the most difficult obstacles.

Furthermore, the act of not giving up can inspire others and create a ripple effect of positivity and determination. By demonstrating resilience and perseverance in the face of adversity, we can serve as a role model for others who may be facing similar challenges. Our ability to overcome obstacles and achieve success can serve as a source of motivation and inspiration for those around us, encouraging them to keep pushing forward and not give up on their own goals and dreams.

The phrase "don't give up" serves as a powerful reminder of the importance of perseverance, resilience, and determination. By refusing to give up in the face of adversity, we can achieve great things, build resilience, and inspire others to do the same. The key to success lies in embracing challenges, learning from setbacks, and pushing through obstacles with a growth mindset. In a world that is constantly changing and evolving, the ability to persevere in the face of adversity is a valuable skill that can lead to personal and professional growth. So, the next time you feel like giving up, remember the importance of resilience and determination, and keep pushing forward towards your goals.

Don't miss out!

Visit the website below and you can sign up to receive emails whenever Daniel Payne publishes a new book. There's no charge and no obligation.

https://books2read.com/r/B-A-WZTCB-YPCXC

BOOKS 2 READ

Connecting independent readers to independent writers.

About the Author

Daniel Payne is a lifelong educator and researcher. He currently lives with his partner and two cats in Chicago, IL.